BARBARY MACAQUE AS PET

LIVING WITH BARBARY MACAQUES AND THE UNIQUE EXPERIENCE OF KEEPING THEM AS PETS

DR HUNTER DAVIS

Table of Contents

Introduction

Often referred to as Barbary apes or Barbary monkeys, Barbary macaques are amazing primates that are indigenous to North Africa's hilly terrain. For millennia, people have been fascinated by Barbary macaques due to their remarkable appearance, social behavior, and intelligence. In recent years, some people have been lured to the idea of keeping Barbary macaques as pets, intrigued by the promise of developing a strong bond with these extraordinary animals.

But keeping a Barbary macaque as a pet is a decision that should not be made hastily. These primates have complex physical, social, and emotional demands that must be properly addressed in captivity to maintain their well-being. Furthermore, there are regional variations in the ethics and legality of owning Barbary macaques as pets, and many areas have stringent laws governing this practice.

We shall examine the nuances of owning Barbary macaques as pets in this extensive tutorial. We will explore every facet of responsible macaque ownership, from comprehending their natural behavior and habitat needs to offering appropriate food, care, and enrichment. Future and present owners of Barbary macaques can have a fulfilling journey of friendship while supporting the welfare of these amazing animals by learning about the special requirements and difficulties of caring for these amazing animals.

Chapter 1

Legal and Ethical Considerations for Owning Barbary Macaques as Pets

The practice of owning Barbary macaques as pets presents serious moral and legal issues. These intelligent and endearing monkeys are native to North Africa, but their complicated requirements make them unfit for domestic pethood. In this thorough examination, we will look at the legal frameworks governing the ownership of Barbary macaques, the ethical implications of keeping them in captivity, and the welfare issues that arise as a result of their status as pets.

- Legal Framework:

The legal status of Barbary macaques varies by country and location. In some locations, possessing a Barbary macaque as a pet is totally forbidden, while in others, there may be laws governing their possession. Before considering purchasing a Barbary macaque as a pet, prospective owners must investigate and understand the rules governing them in their jurisdiction.

One of the main reasons for regulating or prohibiting Barbary macaques as pets is their conservation status. Because of habitat degradation, poaching, and the illicit pet trade, these primates are classified as vulnerable or endangered by groups like the International Union for Conservation of Nature (IUCN). As a result, legislation protecting Barbary macaques in the wild as well as limiting trade and ownership in captivity have been passed in numerous nations.

- Ethical considerations:

Beyond legal problems, there are ethical questions about keeping Barbary macaques as pets. In their native environment, these primates have evolved to live in sophisticated social groupings where they engage in complex behaviors and develop close relationships with other troop members. Captivity denies them the ability to express these natural activities, which can lead to stress, boredom, and psychological discomfort.

Furthermore, the exotic pet trade frequently involves unethical breeding, trafficking, and selling of animals, such as Barbary macaques. Since many of these animals are removed from the wild when they are still young, their social systems are upset and natural populations suffer. Furthermore, the conditions under which captive Barbary macaques are housed may not suit their physical, social, and psychological demands, resulting in poor wellbeing results.

- Welfare Issues:

The welfare of barbary macaques treated as pets is a major problem. These primates require specific care, such as a large and enhanced environment, a diverse and balanced diet, and regular veterinary visits. However, many pet owners may be unable or unwilling to effectively provide these demands, resulting in health difficulties, behavioral concerns, and animal misery.

One of the most important welfare concerns for confined Barbary macaques is inadequate accommodation. These primates are extremely active and intellectual, requiring plenty of room to walk, climb, and explore. Confining them in small cages or enclosures can cause stress, frustration, and the emergence of aberrant behaviors like stereotypies.

The absence of stimulation and sociability is another problem with welfare. Barbary macaques are social animals that live in big groups in the wild. They interact with one another in a complicated way and depend on one another for support and friendship. Pet macaques in captivity may experience loneliness, depression, and anxiety as a result of solitary confinement or insufficient socializing with other macaques.

Moreover, poor nutrition and diet can have an adverse effect on the health and welfare of Barbary macaques kept in captivity. These primates have specialized dietary requirements, which include a wide range of fruits, vegetables, nuts, seeds, and proteins. A diet low in key nutrients or heavy in processed foods can cause nutritional deficiencies, obesity, and other health issues.

To summarize, the legal and ethical implications of keeping Barbary macaques as pets are complex and multifaceted. While certain governments may allow their ownership under specific conditions, the wellbeing of these animals must be prioritized. Barbary macaques must be owned responsibly, which means adhering to legal requirements, ethical standards, and animal care best practices.

Finally, the greatest method to improve Barbary macaques' well-being is to maintain their natural environment, support conservation efforts, and recognize their position as wild creatures. Rather of keeping macaques as pets, people can help to save them by supporting groups that aim to preserve their natural habitats and rehabilitate injured or orphaned macaques for release back into the wild. We can assure a better future for Barbary macaques by putting their welfare and conservation first.

Chapter 2

Understanding the behavior and needs of Barbary macaques.

Barbary macaques, often called Barbary apes or Barbary monkeys, are intriguing primates recognized for their intricate social systems, intelligence, and expressive behaviors. These endearing creatures, who are native to North Africa's hilly regions, have piqued the curiosity of scientists, environmentalists, and enthusiasts alike. We will delve into the complex behaviors and fundamental needs of Barbary macaques in this in-depth investigation, illuminating their natural history, social dynamics, cognitive capacities, and needs for the best possible welfare in captivity.

- Natural History, Habitat:

Barbary macaques are members of the Old World monkey family Cercopithecidae, specifically the genus Macaca. They are one of the few macaque species that live outside of Asia, in the Atlas Mountains of Morocco and Algeria. Barbary macaques live in a range of habitats throughout this harsh terrain, including cedar forests, oak woodlands, and steep cliffs, where they have adapted to different environmental conditions.

These primates are largely arboreal, spending much of their time in trees foraging for food, seeking refuge from predators, and engaging in social activities. They are, nevertheless, capable of terrestrial movement and can roam between feeding places or group territory. Their nimble bodies and prehensile tails allow them to easily explore complicated landscapes, while their excellent senses of sight and hearing aid them in detecting potential predators and resources.

- Social Dynamics and Structure:

Barbary macaques are highly gregarious creatures who form intricate multi-male, multi-female social groups known as troops. Troops are often made up of numerous adult males, multiple adult females, and their progeny, which constitute a cohesive unit with established hierarchies and alliances. Individuals in the troop participate in a range of social behaviors, such as grooming, play, and communication using vocalizations, facial expressions, and body postures.

Barbary macaques' social organization is heavily influenced by dominance hierarchies, with dominant individuals having preferential access to resources and mating opportunities. In addition to agonistic interactions like threats, displays, and physical violence, affiliative behaviors and alliances with other group members can also be used to sustain dominance.

- Reproduction and Family Life:

Barbary macaque troops have different reproductive methods, with dominant males often monopolizing mating opportunities and producing the majority of progeny. However, subordinate males may engage in clandestine matings or form partnerships with females to improve their reproductive success. Female Barbary macaques usually give birth to a single baby following a five to six-month gestation period, with babies relying largely on their mothers for care and safety.

Females receive alloparental care, grooming, and protection from other troop members during infant raising, which is a communal endeavor. Juvenile Barbary macaques go through a period of social learning and development, acquiring important skills and behaviors through observation, imitation, and play. As they reach sexual maturity, young males may leave their natal troop in search of other social chances, although females frequently stay with their birth group.

- Feeding Behavior and Diet:

Barbary macaques are omnivores, eating a wide range of foods based on seasonal availability and local resources. Their diet is mostly composed of fruits, seeds, leaves, flowers, and insects, with occasional vertebrate prey like as small mammals, birds, and reptiles. These primates are opportunistic foragers, consuming a wide variety of food sources within their natural habitat and modifying their diet to changing environmental conditions.

Barbary macaques' foraging behavior is influenced by food availability, competition with other group members, and predation risk. They use a range of eating tactics, such as finding, handling, and processing food items using their nimble hands and advanced manipulation abilities. Barbary macaques may also engage in extractive foraging behaviors, such as digging for roots, breaking nuts, or searching crevices for insects.

- Environmental Enrichment and Cognitive Stimulation:

Barbary macaques in captivity require environmental enrichment and cognitive stimulation to maintain their physical and psychological well-being. Enrichment activities should be consistent with their normal behaviors and habitat preferences, fostering exploration, foraging, social engagement, and problem-solving. Enrichment for captive macaques can take the form of puzzle feeders, climbing structures, sensory stimulation gadgets, and interaction opportunities with conspecifics or suitable species.

Cognitive study has shown that Barbary macaques have exceptional problem-solving abilities, memory skills, and social cognition. They are able to learn difficult activities, recognize individual faces, and comprehend social interactions within their group. Providing opportunities for mental stimulation and social connection is consequently critical for keeping caged macaques' cognitive health and behavioral flexibility intact.

- Health and Veterinary Care:

To ensure the health and welfare of Barbary macaques in captivity, they must have access to appropriate veterinarian treatment and preventative medicine. Regular health screenings, immunizations, and parasite management are critical for preventing and managing infectious diseases that might harm captive macaques. Furthermore, routine dental care, grooming, and body condition monitoring can aid in the prevention of dental disorders, obesity, and other health issues connected with captive life.

Captive macaque care includes behavioral monitoring and management. Recognizing indicators of stress, aggression, or disease and applying appropriate interventions, like as environmental changes or behavioral training, can help to alleviate welfare problems and promote positive adaptation to captive settings. Furthermore, allowing macaques to engage in natural behaviors, socializing with others, and environmental enrichment can improve their general well-being.

To summarize, understanding the behavior and needs of Barbary macaques is critical for their wellbeing and conservation, whether in their natural habitat or in captivity. These extraordinary primates have intricate social structures, cognitive capacities, and adaptive behaviors that reflect their evolutionary history and ecological niche. By honoring their natural behaviors and meeting their physical, social, and psychological needs, we can secure Barbary macaques' well-being and survival for future generations.

Chapter 3

Creating the ideal habitat for your Barbary macaque

Providing an ideal environment for Barbary macaques is critical for fostering their physical and psychological well-being in captivity. Barbary macaques, as highly active and cognitive primates, have special habitat needs that must be satisfied to maintain their health, happiness, and quality of life. In this comprehensive guide, we will look at the important components of creating and maintaining an ideal habitat for Barbary macaques, including enclosure size and layout, environmental enrichment, diet and nutrition, social dynamics, and veterinary care.

- Enclosure Design and Layout:

The foundation of an optimal environment for Barbary macaques is a large and safe enclosure that allows for natural activities, movement, and exploration. The enclosure size should be appropriate to the number of macaques confined within it, with plenty of room for climbing, running, and social contact. Ideally, the cage should have both indoor and outdoor sections to meet the macaques' requirements for shelter, sunlight, and fresh air.

Indoor enclosures should be well-insulated, climate-controlled, and outfitted with suitable flooring and substrate materials to ensure cleanliness and comfort. Naturalistic components like as branches, ropes, platforms, and hammocks can be used to allow for climbing, perching, and relaxing. To encourage mental stimulation and behavioral variety, the enclosure should also have hiding places, nesting materials, and enrichment items.

Outdoor enclosures should be securely walled and designed to resemble the macaques' native habitat, with flora, rocks, and features that promote exploration and foraging. Natural barriers, such as moats or rock formations, can assist discourage escape attempts and reduce conflicts with nearby animals or humans. Access to good water supplies, shade, and shelter from bad weather are critical for macaques' comfort and well-being.

- Enhancement of the Environment:

Environmental enrichment is critical for maintaining the physical and psychological wellbeing of captive Barbary macaques. Enrichment activities should be designed to match the macaques' natural habits and preferences, allowing for exploration, foraging, social contact, and cognitive stimulation. A wide range of enrichment gadgets and strategies can be utilized to improve the macaques' surroundings and stimulate species-typical behaviors.

Food enrichment is an efficient technique to encourage natural foraging activities while also providing mental and physical stimulation to Barbary macaques. Puzzle feeders, scatter feeding, and food-dispensing devices can be used to motivate macaques to work for their food, simulating the difficulties of finding food in the wild. Furthermore, hiding food items in substrates or natural materials can stimulate macaques to use their senses and problem-solving abilities to find and collect them.

Barbary macaques, who are extremely social creatures who thrive on interaction and affection, require social enrichment as well. Allowing macaques to associate with conspecifics or suitable species can help reduce boredom, loneliness, and stress. Fostering grooming interactions, scheduling play sessions, and welcoming new members into the group can all help to build social ties and foster a healthy group dynamic.

Cognitive enrichment entails giving macaques opportunities to engage in mentally stimulating activities and tasks that stretch their cognitive capacities. Training sessions, puzzle toys, and novel things can all help to promote exploration, problem solving, and learning. Additionally, allowing macaques to engage in natural behaviors such as foraging, grooming, and social play can improve their cognitive abilities and mental well-being.

- Diet and nutrition:

Proper feeding is critical to the health and well-being of Barbary macaques in captivity. A well-balanced diet that matches their nutritional needs is essential for long-term health, growth, and reproduction. Captive macaques' diets should closely resemble their wild diets, which include a variety of fruits, vegetables, nuts, seeds, and protein sources.

Barbary macaques require a nutritionally balanced diet that includes a variety of carbs, proteins, fats, vitamins, and minerals. Fresh fruits and vegetables should comprise the majority of their diet, supplemented by nuts, seeds, and protein sources such as eggs, lean meats, or insects. Avoid foods heavy in sugar, salt, or fat, as well as hazardous plants or compounds that could harm macaques.

Feeding methods and timetables should be designed to accommodate the macaques' natural feeding behaviors and preferences, allowing for foraging, manipulation, and social engagement. Food enrichment strategies such as scatter feeding, puzzle feeders, and foraging devices can help to promote natural feeding patterns while preventing boredom or overconsumption.

Veterinary Care and Health Monitoring:

Barbary macaques require regular veterinarian treatment and health monitoring to ensure their well-being in captivity. Routine health checks, immunizations, and parasite management are critical for avoiding and treating infectious diseases that might afflict captive macaques. Furthermore, dental treatment, grooming, and monitoring of physical condition can help prevent dental problems, obesity, and other health issues connected with captive life.

Captive macaque care includes behavioral monitoring and management. Recognizing indicators of stress, aggression, or disease and applying appropriate interventions, like as environmental changes or behavioral training, can help to alleviate welfare problems and promote positive adaptation to captive settings. Additionally, allowing for natural activities, social engagement, and habitat enrichment can improve the general well-being of caged macaques.

To summarize, constructing an ideal habitat for Barbary macaques in captivity necessitates careful consideration of their physical, social, and psychological requirements. We can boost captive macaques' health, happiness, and welfare by providing a roomy and enriched environment that incorporates naturalistic features, allows for foraging and social contact, and ensures sufficient feeding and veterinary treatment. By prioritizing the well-being of these magnificent monkeys, we can help to conserve them and secure a better future for Barbary macaques in captivity and in the wild.

Chapter 4

Food and Nutrition Guidelines for Barbary Macaques

Feeding and nutrition are critical components of caring for captive Barbary macaques. Barbary macaques, as omnivorous primates with different dietary needs, require a well-balanced diet that fits their nutritional needs in order to maintain good health, growth, and well-being. In this detailed guide, we will look at Barbary macaques' feeding patterns, nutritional demands, and dietary issues, as well as provide recommendations for making a healthy and balanced diet for these unique monkeys in captivity.

- Natural diet and foraging behavior:

In the wild, Barbary macaques eat a variety of fruits, seeds, leaves, flowers, insects, and tiny animals. They are opportunistic foragers who use a variety of food sources based on seasonal availability and local resources. Barbary macaques spend a lot of time searching for food in their natural environment, using their agile hands and extensive manipulation skills to find, handle, and process food.

Barbary macaques' foraging behavior is influenced by food availability, competition with other group members, and predation risk. They use a variety of feeding methods, such as looking for, handling, and processing food with their agile bodies and sharp senses. Barbary macaques may also engage in extractive foraging behaviors, such as digging for roots, breaking nuts, or searching crevices for insects.

Understanding Barbary macaques' natural diet and foraging behavior is critical for developing a captive diet that fits their nutritional requirements while encouraging species-typical activities. Caregivers can improve the physical and psychological well-being of caged macaques and prevent diet-related health problems by offering a varied selection of foods as well as opportunities for foraging and manipulation.

- Nutritional requirements:

Barbary macaques have distinct food needs that must be supplied to maintain their health and well-being in captivity. A balanced diet for Barbary macaques should include adequate amounts of carbohydrates, proteins, fats, vitamins, and minerals. To meet these nutritional needs, carefully select and prepare items that replicate the macaques' natural diet in the wild.

Carbohydrates: Carbohydrates are an important source of energy for Barbary macaques, as they fuel their daily activity and metabolism. Complex carbohydrates such as fruits, vegetables, and grains should make up the majority of the macaque's diet, giving fiber, vitamins, and minerals as well as energy.

Proteins: Proteins are required for muscle growth, healing, and maintenance in Barbary macaques. Protein sources in the macaque diet may include nuts, seeds, beans, eggs, lean meats, and insects. It is important to give a range of protein sources to guarantee appropriate consumption of critical amino acids.

Fats provide a concentrated source of energy and vital fatty acids for Barbary macaques. To promote overall health and well-being, macaques should consume healthy fats in moderation, such as those found in nuts, seeds, avocados, and fatty fish.

Barbary macaques require a number of vitamins and minerals to support their growth, development, and immunological function. Fruits and vegetables contain high levels of vitamins A, C, and E, as well as minerals like calcium, potassium, and magnesium. Supplementation may be required to maintain appropriate consumption of specific vitamins and minerals, especially in caged macaques that have restricted access to natural diets.

Water: Barbary macaques require adequate fluids to maintain proper body temperature, digestion, and metabolic functions. Macaques should always have access to fresh, clean water, either from open water sources or by placing water bowls or bottles within their enclosure on a regular basis.

- Feeding guidelines:

Barbary macaques' eating instructions should take into account their natural dietary choices, nutritional needs, and feeding patterns. Caregivers should attempt to provide a well-balanced food that meets these requirements while encouraging species-typical behaviors and reducing diet-related health issues. The guidelines below can help ensure the health and well-being of captive Barbary macaques:

Variety: Provide a varied choice of foods to imitate the macaques' normal diet and supply critical nutrients. Include a variety of fruits, vegetables, nuts, seeds, cereals, and protein sources in the macaque's diet to promote nutritional balance and variation.

Freshness: Serve fresh, high-quality foods that are free of spoilage, mold, and contamination. Rotate food items on a regular basis to avoid boredom and ensure dietary variety, and remove uneaten food from the enclosure to keep it clean and sanitary.

Portions: Provide portion sizes that are appropriate for the macaques' size, age, and activity level. Monitor food intake and body condition on a frequent basis to avoid overfeeding or underfeeding, and alter portion sizes as needed to maintain optimal body condition and health.

Feeding Schedule: Create a consistent feeding schedule that includes several short meals throughout the day to match the macaques' natural eating habits. Monitor feeding behavior and change the feeding schedule as necessary to fit individual preferences and nutritional requirements.

Encourage natural foraging activities by allowing macaques to hunt for, handle, and manipulate food objects. Scatter feeding, puzzle feeders, and foraging devices can serve to stimulate mental and physical activities while avoiding boredom or overconsumption.

Supervision: Keep an eye on feeding sessions to make sure that no dominant individual monopolizes resources and that all macaques have access to food. Having distinct feeding zones or a number of feeding stations might lessen the possibility of rivalry and hostility during mealtimes.

Veterinary Oversight: Work with a veterinarian who specializes in primate care to create a nutritionally balanced diet and feeding plan for Barbary macaques in captivity. Regular health screenings and nutritional assessments can help identify and manage any dietary deficits or health problems that may occur.

Finally, feeding and nutrition are critical components of caring for captive Barbary macaques. Caregivers can construct a balanced diet for captive macaques by researching their natural diet, nutritional requirements, and feeding habits. We can meet the nutritional demands and dietary preferences of Barbary macaques in captivity by providing a choice of fresh, high-quality meals, allowing for foraging and manipulation, and periodically evaluating feeding behavior and body condition.

Chapter 5

Health and veterinary care for barbary macaques

Barbary macaques in captivity require complete veterinarian care as well as preventive medicine to maintain their health and well-being. Barbary macaques, as highly cognitive and social primates, are vulnerable to a wide range of health disorders that can affect their physical, mental, and emotional well-being. In this comprehensive book, we will look at the basics of health and veterinary care for Barbary macaques, including preventative medicine, common health problems, veterinarian examinations, diagnostic methods, treatment choices, and emergency care.

- Preventive Medicine:

Preventive medicine is essential for sustaining the health and well-being of captive Barbary macaques. Caregivers can prevent significant health problems by taking a proactive approach to health care. Vaccinations, parasite control, dental treatment, grooming, and environmental management are all potential preventative interventions for Barbary macaques.

Vaccinations: Infectious diseases that could endanger the health and wellbeing of Barbary macaques must be prevented via vaccinations. Common immunizations for macaques include measles, TB, hepatitis, and influenza. Vaccination schedules should be developed in cooperation with a primate-experienced veterinarian and customized to the macaques' unique needs and dangers in captivity.

Parasite Control: Parasite control is essential for preventing internal and external parasite infestations, which can cause discomfort, illness, and disease in Barbary macaques. Regular deworming, flea and tick prevention, and ectoparasite control treatments should all be included in a comprehensive parasite management program. Caregivers should keep an eye out for indicators of parasite infections in macaques, such as itching, hair loss, or behavioral abnormalities, and seek veterinary care as needed.

Dental Care: Dental care is critical for the oral health and cleanliness of Barbary macaques. Regular dental exams, cleanings, and preventative treatments can help you avoid periodontal disease, tooth rot, and tooth loss. To maintain dental health, avoid boredom or destructive behavior, and improve oral health, caregivers should offer macaques with suitable chew toys, dental snacks, and enrichment activities.

Grooming: A crucial part of keeping Barbary macaques in captivity clean and hygienic is grooming. Regular grooming sessions can help eliminate dirt, debris, and parasites from macaques' fur, skin, and nails, hence minimizing skin infections, matting, and discomfort. In addition to giving macaques access to grooming supplies like combs, brushes, and wipes, caregivers should also construct a stress-free and cozy grooming schedule for the animals.

Environmental Management: Maintaining the health and well-being of Barbary macaques kept in captivity and preventing sickness are major goals of environmental management. Enclosures should be clean, well-ventilated, and free of potential risks including sharp objects, hazardous plants, and severe temperatures. Regular maintenance and sanitation measures should be performed to ensure that the macaques' living area is clean and safe.

- Common Health Issues:

Barbary macaques are prone to a number of health problems that can harm their physical and emotional well-being. Understanding the common health problems that might emerge in captive macaques is critical for early detection, diagnosis, and treatment. Some of the most prevalent health conditions in Barbary macaques could include:

Captive macaques are prone to respiratory illnesses, which can be caused by bacteria, viruses, or other diseases. Symptoms may include coughing, sneezing, nasal discharge, tiredness, and difficulty breathing. Prompt veterinarian treatment with antibiotics, supportive care, and environmental management are required to treat respiratory infections and prevent their spread within the group.

Gastrointestinal Disorders: Barbary macaques may have diarrhea, vomiting, and gastrointestinal pain as a result of food indiscretion, infectious agents, or underlying health issues. Caregivers should keep an eye on macaques' appetite, bowel movements, and demeanor, and seek veterinary care if gastrointestinal issues persist or worsen.

Dermatological Issues: Skin infections, allergies, and parasitic infestations can all cause discomfort and irritation in Barbary macaques. Itching, redness, hair loss, and skin lesions are among the possible symptoms. To ease dermatological disorders and enhance skin health, veterinarians may prescribe topical or systemic drugs, parasite control techniques, and environmental adjustments.

Periodontal disease, tooth decay, and dental abscesses are examples of dental disorders that Barbary macaques might develop as a result of poor oral hygiene, nutritional variables, or genetic susceptibility. Caregivers should keep an eye out for indicators of dental difficulties in macaques, such as foul breath, drooling, or a refusal to feed, and seek veterinary care as needed to manage tooth concerns and avoid further consequences.

Reproductive Health Issues: Female Barbary macaques may experience infertility, reproductive tract infections, and perinatal problems, whilst males may experience testicular issues or reproductive diseases. Regular reproductive health examinations and monitoring are critical for detecting and treating reproductive health disorders in confined macaques, as well as increasing overall reproductive success and well-being.

- Veterinary Examination and Diagnostic Procedures:

Veterinary examinations and diagnostic procedures are required to assess the health state, diagnose health problems, and design treatment strategies for Barbary macaques in captivity. Regular veterinary examinations should be performed by a veterinarian experienced in primate care, and may include:

Physical examinations entail a complete evaluation of the macaques' entire health, including body condition, vital signs, and physical appearance. Veterinarians may palpate the macaques' tummy, chest, and limbs to look for anomalies or symptoms of pain or distress.

Diagnostic tests, such as bloodwork, urinalysis, fecal examinations, and imaging studies, may be used to check the macaques' internal health and identify underlying health disorders. Blood tests can reveal important information about macaques' hematological and biochemical parameters, whereas urine and fecal investigations can detect signs of infection, inflammation, or parasitic infestations.

Behavioral Assessments: Behavioral assessments can be used to assess the macaques' mental and emotional well-being and identify any indicators of stress, anxiety, or behavioral problems. Observations of macaques' behavior in their social group and interactions with caregivers might reveal important information about their psychological health and welfare.

- Treatment Options and Medication:

Treatment solutions for health problems in Barbary macaques may differ based on the nature and severity of the ailment. In order to treat health conditions and aid in rehabilitation, veterinarians may perform surgical operations, write prescriptions for drugs, or suggest supportive care measures. The following are some typical therapies for medical conditions affecting Barbary macaques:

Antibiotics can be used to treat bacterial infections in Barbary macaques, such as respiratory infections, skin infections, or urinary tract infections. Caregivers should administer antibiotics as prescribed by a veterinarian and monitor the macaques' response to treatment for signs of improvement or adverse reactions.

Antiparasitic Medications: Anthelmintics, antiprotozoals, and ectoparasiticides may be used to treat internal and external parasitic infections in Barbary macaques. Caregivers should administer antiparasitic drugs according to the veterinarian's instructions and keep an eye out for indicators of parasite clearance or recurrence in macaques.

Anti-inflammatory Drugs: Anti-inflammatory drugs such as nonsteroidal anti-inflammatory drugs (NSAIDs) or corticosteroids may be prescribed to alleviate pain, inflammation, or swelling associated with health issues such as arthritis, dermatitis, or soft tissue injuries in Barbary macaques. Caregivers should administer anti-inflammatory drugs with caution and monitor the macaques for potential side effects or adverse reactions.

Surgical Procedures: Surgical procedures may be performed to address health issues such as dental problems, reproductive disorders, or traumatic injuries in Barbary macaques. Caregivers should follow postoperative care recommendations provided by the veterinarian and monitor the macaques for evidence of surgical complications or delayed recovery.

Supportive Care: During illness or injury, Barbary macaques may benefit from supportive care interventions such as dietary support, hydration treatment, and environmental changes. These interventions can aid in the animals' rehabilitation and overall wellbeing. As instructed by the doctor, caregivers should provide the macaques the proper supportive care and keep an eye out for any indications of improvement or decline in the animal's response to treatment.

- Emergency Care:

Emergency care is crucial for resolving acute health issues, traumatic injuries, or life-threatening conditions in Barbary macaques. Caregivers should be prepared to respond swiftly to emergencies and seek veterinarian assistance as needed to stabilize the macaques' condition and offer appropriate medical treatment. Some common emergency circumstances in Barbary macaques may include:

Respiratory Distress: Respiratory distress can occur in Barbary macaques due to illnesses such as pneumonia, bronchitis, or airway obstruction. Caregivers should monitor the macaques for signs of trouble breathing, cyanosis, or gasping and seek veterinary aid quickly to handle respiratory emergencies and offer supportive care.

Traumatic Injuries: Traumatic injuries such as wounds, fractures, or lacerations can develop in Barbary macaques due to accidents, fights, or falls. Caregivers should determine the degree of the damage, control bleeding, and administer first aid procedures such as wound cleaning and bandaging while obtaining veterinary assistance for further diagnosis and treatment.

Toxicity: Toxicity can occur in Barbary macaques owing to intake of harmful plants, chemicals, or substances.

Caregivers should detect and remove probable poisons from the macaques' habitat, induce vomiting if necessary, and seek veterinary assistance immediately for supportive care and treatment of poisoning symptoms.

Seizures: Seizures can occur in Barbary macaques due to illnesses such as epilepsy, metabolic abnormalities, or toxic exposures. Caregivers should safeguard the safety of the macaques during seizures, protect them from injury, and seek veterinary assistance swiftly to diagnose the underlying cause of seizures and provide appropriate medical therapy.

In conclusion, health and veterinary care are vital components of caring for Barbary macaques in captivity. By implementing preventive measures, conducting regular veterinary checkups, and managing health issues promptly and efficiently, caretakers can ensure the health, well-being, and lifespan of captive macaques. By focusing the physical and emotional health of Barbary macaques, we may enhance their overall welfare and contribute to their conservation and survival for future generations.

Chapter 6

Enrichment Activities and Mental Stimulation for Barbary Macaques

Enrichment activities and mental stimulation are vital for promoting the physical, cognitive, and emotional well-being of Barbary macaques in captivity. As extremely clever and gregarious primates, Barbary macaques thrive on opportunities for exploration, problem-solving, and social contact. In this thorough book, we will investigate the principles of enrichment and mental stimulation for Barbary macaques, covering a wide range of activities and ways to enhance their captive habitat and support their natural behaviors and psychological needs.

- Understanding Barbary Macaque Behavior:

Before developing enrichment activities for Barbary macaques, it is vital to understand their natural habits and preferences. In the wild, Barbary macaques engage in a variety of behaviors such as foraging, grooming, socializing, climbing, and playing. These actions are adaptive responses to their natural environment and serve crucial tasks like as getting food, establishing social relationships, and avoiding predators.

In captivity, Barbary macaques may exhibit stereotypic behaviors such as pacing, rocking, or self-injurious behaviors if their environmental and social demands are not adequately addressed. Stereotypic behaviors are often an indication of stress, dissatisfaction, or boredom and may suggest that the macaques' captive habitat lacks appropriate stimulation or opportunity for natural behaviors.

- Enrichment Principles:

Enrichment for Barbary macaques should be tailored to improve their physical, cognitive, and emotional well-being by offering opportunity for natural behaviors, social contact, and cerebral stimulation. The following concepts can guide the construction of effective enrichment programs for Barbary macaques:

Variety: Offer a diversified choice of enrichment activities and materials to stimulate multiple senses and create unique experiences for the macaques. Enrichment should include opportunities for foraging, climbing, manipulation, social engagement, and cognitive challenge to suit the macaques' broad behavioral and psychological needs.

Choice: Allow macaques to choose how they engage with enrichment activities and materials, respecting their individual preferences and autonomy. Offer several enrichment alternatives within their cage and enable them to explore, engage, and manipulate enrichment objects at their own pace and in their own way.

Novelty: Introduce novel enrichment activities and materials often to prevent habituation and preserve the macaques' interest and involvement. Novelty encourages interest and exploration, encouraging the macaques to study and engage with their environment and enrichment objects.

effort: Provide enrichment activities that offer a level of effort and complexity relevant to the macaques' cognitive talents and experience. Challenging tasks foster problem-solving, investigation, and learning, promoting mental stimulation and behavioral adaptability.

Safety: Ensure that enrichment activities and materials are safe for macaques to interact with and free from potential hazards such as sharp edges, small parts, or toxic substances. Monitor enrichment items routinely for signs of wear or damage and replace them as needed to preserve safety and efficacy.

- Enrichment Activities:

There are many various forms of enrichment activities that can be provided for Barbary macaques, ranging from food-based puzzles to social interactions with caregivers. The idea is to give a variety of activities that excite the macaques' physical, cognitive, and social talents and foster species-typical behaviors. Some examples of enrichment activities for Barbary macaques include:

Food Enrichment: Food enrichment is offering food in unique or challenging ways to enhance natural foraging habits and mental stimulation. Examples of food enrichment for Barbary macaques may include puzzle feeders, scatter feeding, food-dispensing toys, frozen treats, or hiding food items within substrates or enrichment devices.

Cognitive Enrichment: Cognitive enrichment activities entail exposing macaques with tasks or puzzles that demand problem-solving, memory, and learning. Examples of cognitive enrichment for Barbary macaques may include training sessions, puzzle toys, object manipulation tasks, or tasks that require macaques to utilize tools or perform sequences of behaviors to gain a reward.

Social Enrichment: Social enrichment activities comprise providing macaques with opportunity for social engagement, play, and communication with conspecifics or suitable species. Examples of social enrichment for Barbary macaques may include introducing new people to the group, planning play sessions, offering grooming opportunities, or rotating macaques between other social groups or enclosures.

Physical Enrichment: Physical enrichment activities comprise giving macaques with opportunity for physical activity, exploration, and motility. Examples of physical enrichment for Barbary macaques may include climbing structures, ropes, swings, tunnels, or platforms that encourage natural behaviors such as climbing, jumping, swinging, or balancing.

Sensory Enrichment: Sensory enrichment exercises entail activating the macaques' senses of sight, hearing, smell, taste, and touch to provide various sensory experiences and environmental stimulation. Examples of sensory enrichment for Barbary macaques may include offering novel odors, sounds, textures, or visual stimuli within their cage or introducing them to new surroundings or sensory experiences outside of their habitat.

- Enrichment Implementation:

Implementing enrichment activities for Barbary macaques involves careful planning, observation, and evaluation to assure effectiveness and safety. Caregivers should consider the specific preferences, abilities, and requirements of the macaques while creating and conducting enrichment programs and be prepared to change activities based on their response and input. The following steps can help guide the execution of enrichment activities for Barbary macaques:

Assessment: Assess the macaques' existing enrichment needs and preferences by behavioral observations, enrichment inventories, and consultation with expert caretakers or primatologists. Identify places where enrichment might be increased or expanded to better suit the macaques' behavioral and psychological demands.

Planning: Develop a comprehensive enrichment plan that includes a variety of activities and materials geared to the macaques' individual and group needs. Consider characteristics such as age, sex, social dynamics, health status, and past enrichment experiences while arranging enrichment activities.

Implementation: Implement enrichment activities according to the enrichment plan, offering chances for macaques to engage with enrichment objects and materials on a regular basis. Monitor the macaques' behavior and interactions with enrichment objects, making adjustments as needed to enhance engagement and prevent habituation.

Evaluation: Evaluate the success of enrichment programs through regular behavioral observations, enrichment records, and input from caretakers and veterinary professionals. Assess the macaques' response to enrichment activities, changes in behavior, and measures of well-being to determine the influence of enrichment on their physical, cognitive, and emotional health.

Modification: Modify enrichment activities and materials as needed based on the macaques' response and feedback, making tweaks to encourage engagement, challenge, and variety. Introduce new enrichment items, rotate old ones, or adjust the presentation or complexity of enrichment tasks to maintain interest and efficacy over time.

In conclusion, enrichment activities and mental stimulation are vital for enhancing the health, well-being, and welfare of Barbary macaques in captivity. By offering opportunities for natural activities, social connection, and cognitive challenge, caretakers can enhance the macaques' captive habitat and support their physical, cognitive, and emotional requirements. By adopting enrichment activities that are varied, interesting, and suited to the macaques' particular preferences and talents, we can improve their lives and promote their overall wellbeing and quality of life in captivity.

Chapter 7

Educating and Developing a Bond with Your Barbary Macaque

Forming a close bond with your Barbary macaque via training not only improves the relationship between caregiver and primate, but it also helps the macaque receive mental and physical stimulation as well as general health benefits. The fundamentals of training and bonding with Barbary macaques will be covered in this comprehensive guide, along with methods, advantages, safety precautions, and the significance of positive reinforcement.

- Recognizing the Behavior of Barbary Macaques:

It's important to comprehend Barbary macaques' behavior, communication, and social structure before beginning any kind of training. Barbary macaques are clever, extremely gregarious monkeys with intricate social structures and communication networks. They use a variety of behaviors, such as grooming, playing, foraging, and vocalizing, to interact with other members of their group and to find their way about.

- Goals for Training:

Training goals for Barbary macaques might change based on the demands of the particular animal as well as the caregiver's objectives. Nonetheless, typical training goals include of:

- building rapport and trust between the macaque and the caregiver.
- encouraging positive actions, including cooperating with veterinary examinations or farm tasks.
- delivering enrichment and mental stimulation through interactive training sessions.

- enhancing the physical activity and mental stimulation of macaques to improve their quality of life in captivity.

- encouraging actions like offering body parts for inspection or willingly taking medicines to help with medical care and management.

- preparing macaques to take part in scientific research or educational displays in order to support conservation and research initiatives.

- Methods of Training:

For training Barbary macaques, positive reinforcement training is the most popular and successful approach. Using a positive reinforcement method like food, praise, or play, this technique aims to make desired behaviors more likely to occur again in the future. The fundamental ideas and methods of positive reinforcement training are as follows:

Operant Conditioning: Operant conditioning is the process of molding behavior by using rewards or penalties. Punishment reduces a behavior's likelihood of recurring, but positive reinforcement enhances it. Positive reinforcement is the main tool used in training Barbary macaques to promote desirable actions.

Clicker Training: A type of operant conditioning, clicker training uses a unique sound produced by a handheld clicker device to let the macaque know when it has correctly executed the intended behavior. During training sessions, the clicker facilitates explicit communication and timing between the behavior and the reward.

Target Training: Using a particular body part, usually the nose or hand, target training teaches the macaque to touch or follow a marked object, like a stick or ball. Target training offers a flexible basis for more intricate training tasks and can be used to teach a wide range of behaviors, such as body posture, recall, and stationing.

Desensitization and Counterconditioning: Macaques can be assisted in overcoming fears or anxiety related to particular stimuli or situations by using desensitization and counterconditioning techniques. Caretakers can assist the macaque learn to identify the feared stimuli with positive outcomes and eventually lessen its fear reaction by introducing it to it gradually in a regulated and positive way and coupling it with rewards or enjoyable experiences.

Shaping is the process of rewarding progressively closer approximations of a desired behavior until the desired behavior is attained. Using a series of approximations, caregivers begin by rewarding any behavior that even slightly approaches the target behavior and work their way up to the intended final behavior. Training becomes more attainable for the macaque when intricate behaviors are divided into smaller, more manageable steps thanks to shaping.

- Advantages of Bonding and Training:

There are several advantages to training and developing a relationship with your Barbary macaque for both the caregiver and the primate:

Strengthening the Bond: Training gives caregivers and macaques the chance to engage and communicate positively, which strengthens their relationship and fosters mutual respect and trust.

Mental Stimulation: Through interactive games and problem-solving exercises, training engages the macaque's cognitive faculties and provides mental stimulation and enrichment.

Physical Activity: A lot of training behaviors include physical activity, including running, jumping, or climbing, which gives the macaque important exercise and improves their physical health and fitness.

Veterinary Care: By actively facilitating medical care and management, such as offering body parts for examination or taking medication, trained behaviors help to reduce stress and discomfort during veterinary operations.

Behavioral Management: By teaching substitute, incompatible behaviors and offering outlets for innate tendencies and energies, training can help with behavioral problems or challenges.

Education & Public Outreach: Trained macaques can act as representatives of their species, taking part in public outreach events or educational displays to increase awareness of primate care and conservation.

* Safety and Training Considerations:

Prioritizing the safety and wellbeing of both the caregiver and the primate is crucial when training and developing a bond with Barbary macaques. It is important to take into mind the following factors:

Positive Reinforcement: When training Barbary macaques, never employ unpleasant methods or punishment as these can incite fear, tension, or hostility. Instead, always use positive reinforcement approaches.

Tailored Approach: Acknowledge that every macaque is distinct and could react differently to various training methods and stimuli. Adapt training techniques to the learner's preferences, personality, and learning style.

Persistence and Patience: Training requires consistency, patience, and time. Be ready to devote time and energy to developing a rapport based on trust and progressively molding desired behaviors over the course of several training sessions.

Safety Procedures: Use safety procedures and safety measures, such as using protective gear, securing training sites, and setting up boundaries and clear communication with the macaque, to reduce dangers during training sessions.

Observation and Assessment: Keep a careful eye on the macaque's behavior and reaction to training sessions, and watch out for any indications of stress, annoyance, or discomfort. As necessary, modify surroundings or training techniques to guarantee the welfare and well-being of the macaque.

Professional Advice: If necessary, seek advice and assistance from behaviorists, seasoned trainers, or veterinarians with knowledge of primate health and training. Training sessions can be carried out in a safe, efficient, and morally responsible manner with the support of expert guidance and mentoring.

- Training Activities and Illustrations:

Positive reinforcement strategies can be used to teach Barbary macaques a variety of behaviors and training exercises. Among the instances are:

Target training involves teaching a macaque to touch or follow a predetermined target with its nose or hand. Over time, the behavior can be gradually shaped to target other body parts or objects.

Stationing: Use positive reinforcement to teach the macaque to stay for a predetermined amount of time in a given location or on a particular perch or platform.

Recall: Reward the macaque for willingly coming back to the caregiver by teaching it to come when called by name or by using a particular cue.

Body Presentation: Using positive reinforcement to promote cooperation, teach the macaque to present particular body parts, like its hand, foot, or ear, for inspection or grooming.

Husbandry activities: Using positive reinforcement to lessen the stress and anxiety associated with these procedures, teach the macaque to actively participate in husbandry activities like going into a transport crate, getting shots or medication, or letting its teeth be brushed.

Aside from strengthening the tie between caregiver and primate, training and connecting with your Barbary macaque can also provide mental stimulation, physical activity, and the macaque's general well-being. Caregivers can improve the quality of life for their macaque in captivity by strengthening their relationship with the animal, use positive reinforcement techniques, adjusting training methods to the needs of the individual, putting safety and welfare first, and obtaining professional assistance when necessary. By giving macaques chances for learning, enrichment, and constructive interaction through training, we can promote their welfare and conservation for future generations while also helping people gain a deeper understanding and appreciation of these amazing primates.

Chapter 8

Typical Problems and Fixes for Owning Pet Barbary Macaques

Because of their intricate social, behavioral, and physiological requirements, owning Barbary macaques as pets comes with special problems. Barbary macaques are charming and intelligent, but they need specific habitats and care to be happy in captivity. This thorough guide will go over the typical problems that pet owners and caregivers of Barbary macaques deal with, as well as workable strategies to solve these problems and protect the welfare of these amazing monkeys.

- Recognizing the Needs and Behavior of Barbary Macaques:

Understanding Barbary macaques' normal behavior and demands is crucial before taking on particular tasks.

Barbary macaques are highly intelligent and gregarious primates who do best in settings that allow them to engage in activities common to their species, such as climbing, grooming, and foraging, as well as mental and physical stimulation. Insufficient cerebral stimulation, environmental enrichment, and proper socialization can result in boredom, tension, and behavioral issues in macaques kept in captivity.

- Typical Problems and Their Fixes:

Social Detachment:

- Challenge: In the wild, barbary macaques live in intricate social groups because they are gregarious animals. They could suffer from behavioral problems, depression, and loneliness if they are kept in isolation or don't receive enough socialization.

- Solution: Whenever possible, provide Barbary macaques the chance to socialize with other members of their own species or conspecifics. To meet their social requirements, think about getting them a companion macaque or setting up supervised playdates with other monkeys.

Too Small of an Enclosure:

- Problem: Because barbary macaques are enthusiastic climbers, they need large enclosures with plenty of vertical area for swinging, climbing, and exploring. Enclosures that are too small or badly built might cause physical health issues, boredom, and frustration.

- Solution: To enable macaques to participate in natural activities and physical exercise, provide them with a spacious and well-equipped enclosure that has plenty of climbing frames, platforms, ropes, and branches. Make sure the enclosure satisfies or surpasses the suggested space requirements for macaque species, is safe, and cannot be escaped from.

Insufficient Mental Stimulation

- Challenge: To avoid boredom and foster psychological well-being, barbary macaques—intelligent animals—need mental stimulation and enrichment. In the absence of suitable enrichment, they could display aggressive or stereotypical behaviors, or they might self-harm.

- Solution: Use a range of enrichment tools and activities to stimulate natural behaviors, stimulate the macaques' senses, and provide them cognitive challenges. To pique their interest and develop their problem-solving abilities, provide interactive toys, puzzle feeders, foraging opportunities, and unfamiliar objects.

Inappropriate Nutrition and Diet:

- Challenge: Providing a healthy, well-balanced diet is crucial for Barbary macaques' overall health and wellbeing. An improper or inadequate diet can cause obesity, gastrointestinal disorders, dental difficulties, and malnutrition.

- Solution: To create a meal plan that suits the macaques' nutritional demands depending on their age, sex, activity level, and health state, see a veterinarian or qualified nutritionist for primates. Give a range of fresh produce, leafy greens, nuts, seeds, and protein sources; do not give sweets that are heavy in fat or sugar.

Behavioral Problems:

- Challenge: If the social, environmental, or psychological needs of barbary macaques are not sufficiently addressed in captivity, they may display behavioral problems such aggression, stereotyping, or destructiveness.

- Solution: Use socializing, positive reinforcement training, and environmental enrichment to address the root causes of behavioral problems. To keep people from being bored or frustrated, give them opportunities for physical activity, cerebral stimulation, and outlets for their natural tendencies. To create plans and tactics for behavior modification and management, consult with a trained animal behaviorist or specialist in primate behavior.

- Veterinary Treatment and Health Administration: Managing the health of Barbary macaques in captivity and providing proper veterinary treatment can be difficult because of their predisposition to infectious diseases, dental difficulties, and stress-related health issues.

Solution: Create a proactive veterinary care schedule that consists of routine dental care, immunizations, parasite control, and health examinations. Keep a watchful eye on the macaques' well-being and behavior for any indications of disease or harm, and seek immediate veterinarian care when necessary. To address any health issues as soon as they arise, keep thorough medical records and stay in close contact with your veterinarian.

A Legal and Ethical Perspective:

- Challenge: Depending on your location and the conservation status of the species, owning Barbary macaques as pets may be subject to legal limitations, permissions, or rules.

- Solution: Learn about and abide by all applicable local, state, federal, and international laws and rules regarding the ownership, custody, and transportation of Barbary macaques. Make sure you have all the necessary permissions and permits, and that the macaques you own were obtained lawfully and from reliable sources that place a high priority on animal conservation and welfare.

Although owning a Barbary macaque as a pet has many benefits, there are also big obligations and difficulties involved. Pet owners and caregivers may guarantee the welfare and well-being of these amazing monkeys in captivity by being aware of the natural behavior and needs of Barbary macaques and putting proper care and management strategies into effect. Fostering a healthy and enriching environment for Barbary macaques as pets requires tackling common issues with workable solutions, from socializing and mental stimulation to assuring enough diet and veterinary care.

Chapter 9

FAQs Regarding Pet Barbary Macaques

Primate enthusiasts, barbary macaques are renowned for their social graces, intellect, and endearing dispositions. But having a Barbary macaque as a pet entails a number of duties and considerations. We'll answer often asked questions (FAQs) on the upkeep, behavior, laws, and moral dilemmas surrounding the ownership of Barbary macaques in this book.

- Why are Barbary macaques so popular as pets, and what are they?

Old World monkeys known as barbary macaques (Macaca sylvanus) are indigenous to Gibraltar and the Atlas Mountains in North Africa. Their remarkable appearance, expressive expressions, and intricate social structures are well-known characteristics. Because of their cleverness, ability to adjust to life in captivity, and charming dispositions, barbary macaques are a popular choice for pets.

- Are Barbary macaques good companion animals?

Barbary macaques are not the best pets for most people, despite the fact that they may develop close relationships with people and display playful and loving characteristics. To thrive in captivity, they need specialized care, big, enriched enclosures, mental stimulation, and social connection with other conspecifics. Additionally, due to welfare and conservation issues, owning a Barbary macaque may be prohibited or banned in many places.

- How much does it cost to legally possess a Barbary macaque as a pet?

Depending on your area and local laws, keeping a Barbary macaque as a pet may or may not be permissible. Barbary macaques are legally protected in many nations, including those in the European Union, albeit ownership may be restricted by licenses, permits, or other requirements. It's crucial to learn about and abide by any applicable laws and rules in your area that control the ownership and possession of exotic animals.

- What kind of enclosure and habitat are necessary for Barbary macaques?

Large, well-furnished enclosures that imitate their native environment and offer chances for climbing, swinging, foraging, and socializing are necessary for barbary macaques. Enclosures should ideally have climbing frames, platforms, branches, ropes, hiding places, and equipment for enhancing the environment. A secure, escape-proof enclosure that can suit the macaques' physical and behavioral needs should be provided.

- What should be included in Barbary macaques' food, and how should it be maintained?

The food of barbary macaques, who are omnivores, consists of fruits, vegetables, nuts, seeds, leaves, insects, and sometimes small animals. Their diet in captivity should be diverse and well-balanced to satisfy their unique nutritional needs. Create a meal plan with a range of fresh, natural foods and little processed or high-sugar snacks by consulting with a veterinarian or primate nutritionist.

- How are Barbary macaques to be socialized and handled?

Being gregarious creatures, barbary macaques derive great pleasure from interacting with both human caretakers and other conspecifics. In addition to monitored interaction with human caretakers, macaques held in captivity should have opportunities for positive socialization and involvement with other macaques. To establish rapport and trust with the macaques, it's critical to respect their boundaries and use positive reinforcement in communication.

- What typical behavioral problems do captive Barbary macaques face?

In captivity, stereotyped actions, aggression, self-harm, and destructive behaviors are common behavioral problems in Barbary macaques. These problems frequently result from insufficient mental stimulation, environmental enrichment, or socialization. Finding the root causes of these problems, putting in place suitable enrichment and management techniques, and getting expert advice from qualified veterinarians or primate behaviorists are all necessary to resolve these problems.

- What sort of veterinarian care are needed for Barbary macaques?

For the duration of their captivity, barbary macaques need routine veterinarian care to ensure their health and wellbeing. Regular check-ups, immunizations, dental care, parasite management, and medical issues or injury treatment are all examples of veterinary care. It is imperative that you create a proactive health management plan for your macaques and collaborate with a veterinarian skilled in primate care.

- How can I give my Barbary macaques mental enrichment and stimulation?

For the sake of the wellbeing and general health of Barbary macaques kept in captivity, mental enrichment and stimulation are vital. Puzzle feeders, foraging possibilities, climbing structures, conspecific social interaction, training sessions, and environmental enrichment devices are a few examples of enrichment activities. Offering a range of enrichment activities that stimulate the macaques' senses, support their natural behaviors, and give them with cognitive challenges is crucial.

- Do you have any ethical questions about owning Barbary macaques as pets?

Indeed, owning Barbary macaques as pets raises a number of ethical questions. These include worries about the well-being and standard of living of the macaques kept in captivity, the harm that illegal trade and habitat loss do to wild populations, and the possibility of human-primate zoonotic disease transmission. It is imperative that those who care for and own pets put their macaques' welfare first, follow the law and morality, and promote conservation and responsible pet ownership.

Having a Barbary macaque as a pet is a difficult and demanding duty that calls for understanding of the needs and behavior of the animal as well as careful thought and dedication. Barbary macaques are not good pets for everyone, despite the fact that they can develop close relationships with human caretakers and display endearing and playful characteristics. Before making a choice, prospective owners should carefully consider the care needs, legal requirements, and moral ramifications of having a Barbary macaque. Pet owners may guarantee the health, welfare, and well-being of their Barbary macaques in captivity while supporting conservation efforts and ethical ownership practices by giving them the proper care, socialization, enrichment, and medical attention.

Final Thoughts: Having a Happy Bond with Your Barbary Macaque

Getting a Barbary macaque is more than just owning an exotic pet; it's about starting a path of understanding, enrichment, and companionship. You may create a happy, companionable connection with your Barbary macaque that fosters a greater respect for these amazing primates by being committed, patient, and providing competent care. As we get to the end of our discussion on owning a Barbary macaque, let's consider some important factors to make sure you and your monkey friend have a happy and fulfilling relationship.

- Recognizing and Valuing Their Nature:

Gaining an appreciation for your Barbary macaque's innate habits, instincts, and social dynamics is essential to building a meaningful relationship with them. These primates are gregarious, highly intellectual, expressive animals with intricate needs and feelings. You can establish connection and trust with your macaque partner by paying attention to their behavior, picking up on their cues, and appreciating their uniqueness.

- **Establishing a Richer Setting:**

Your Barbary macaque's physical, mental, and emotional health depend on you providing an enriching environment. Invest in an expansive and engaging enclosure that provides chances for exploration, climbing, foraging, and socializing. Puzzle feeders, interactive toys, and training sessions are examples of enrichment activities that stimulate the mind, encourage natural behaviors, and improve the relationship between you and your macaque.

- **Giving Socialization and Interaction First Priority:**

Social connection between conspecifics and human caregivers is essential for the well-being of barbary macaques. Provide opportunities for supervised engagement with yourself and your family members and for pleasant socializing with other macaques. Developing a relationship with your macaque companion that is founded on mutual respect, trust, and positive reinforcement improves mutual understanding, cooperation, and communication.

- Providing Veterinary Care and a Nutritious Diet:
For the sake of your Barbary macaque's health and wellbeing, make sure they eat a good, well-balanced diet. Consult a nutritionist for primates or a veterinarian to create a feeding plan that is customized to your macaque's individual requirements and tastes. Maintaining the health and lifespan of your macaque requires routine veterinarian exams, immunizations, management of parasites, and fast medical attention for any problems.

- Promoting Enrichment and Stimulation of the Mind:

Enrichment activities and training sessions are essential for your macaque's mental stimulation and overall well-being. Provide a range of learning tools, games, and puzzles that test their ability to solve problems, promote curiosity, and stimulate their senses. Training with positive reinforcement improves communication, fortifies your relationship, and gives your animal the ability to take an active role in their own care and welfare.

- Honoring Ethical and Legal Considerations

Being a responsible owner of a Barbary macaque means abiding by the laws and moral principles pertaining to the ownership and care of exotic animals. Learn about the rules and legislation that apply to owning Barbary macaques in your area, get any licenses or permissions that are required, and promote responsible ownership and conservation. You can support macaque conservation and the survival of their species for future generations by putting their welfare first and honoring their natural heritage.

- Accepting the Benefits and Difficulties:

Taking care of a Barbary macaque is an exciting and demanding undertaking that calls for perseverance, devotion, and continuous education. Accept the pleasures of friendship, the amazement of seeing them in their natural habitat, and the sense of satisfaction that comes from giving them a happy life in captivity. Simultaneously, be ready to take on new tasks, ask for help when necessary, and never stop working to provide your macaque partner with better care and enrichment.

To sum up, having a happy relationship with your Barbary macaque involves learning, showing compassion, and developing both of you. You can develop a relationship that benefits both of your lives by acknowledging their nature, giving them a loving atmosphere, emphasizing socialization and enrichment, and adhering to moral and legal obligations. Savor the times you spend with, acknowledge their uniqueness, and make a commitment to treat your Barbary macaque friend with care. You can go out on a lifetime adventure of friendship and mutual enrichment together.

www.ingramcontent.com/pod-product-compliance
Lightning Source LLC
Chambersburg PA
CBHW051825250726

48659CB00005B/1682